50 Great Sandwiches

STEP-BY-STEP
50 Great Sandwiches

Carole Handslip

Photography by Edward Allwright

CLB 4251

This edition published for
Colour Library Books Ltd
Godalming Business Centre
Woolsack Way
Godalming
Surrey GU7 1XW

© Anness Publishing Limited 1994
Boundary Row Studios
1 Boundary Row
London SE1 8HP

ISBN 1 85833 195 1

Editorial Director: Joanna Lorenz
Series Editor: Lindsay Porter
Designer: Peter Laws
Photographer: Edward Allwright
Stylist: Hilary Guy

Printed and bound in Italy by Graphicom S.r.l., Vicenza

MEASUREMENTS
*Three sets of equivalent measurements have been provided in the recipes here, in the following
order: Metric, Imperial and American. It is essential that units of measurement are not mixed
within each recipe. Where conversions result in awkward numbers, these have been rounded for
convenience, but are accurate enough to produce successful results.*

CONTENTS

INTRODUCTION

The sandwich is said to have been originated in England by the Earl of that name. The fourth Earl of Sandwich (1718–92) was a keen gambler, and so as not to waste time eating away from the gaming tables, he asked to have cold beef placed between two slices of bread in order to continue playing while eating. This very convenient manner of taking sustaining nourishment quickly became popular, and in deference to its inventor became known as the 'sandwich'.

Though the basic idea has remained the same for more than two hundred years, there are now many permutations. The variety and availability of different and excellent breads is enormous, and ideas for fillings abound throughout the world. Each country has its own particular way of preparing this quick and easy snack. In Spain they make *bocadillas*, long rolls stuffed with Serrano ham. In Italy *bruschetta* is a toasted, peasant bread lavishly spread with garlic, olive oil and sometimes tomato. In northern Europe, Germany offers black or rye breads with smoky Westphalia ham. Scandinavia uses pumpernickel with many varieties of herring. From America we have triple-decker club sandwiches and torpedo rolls filled to bursting, called 'heroes', designed to satisfy an heroic appetite! From the East come tikka, satay and other hot, spicy goodies which can be stuffed into pitta bread or simply wrapped in naan – the variety is endless.

In this book are recipes ideal to pack for picnics or to make a lunch box more interesting; there are some super surprises for a children's tea party; and recipes that provide inviting tasty food for the unexpected visitor. When it's just too late to prepare a full cooked meal, a piece of bread with butter and a little of what you fancy will provide a noble supper crust.

Seasonings

Sandwiches are essentially quick and easy, and are often presented as a meal; it is therefore sensible to maintain a well-stocked store-cupboard and refrigerator, so that you can rustle up a satisfying snack at a moment's notice. Such things as tuna fish, anchovies, olives, rollmops, good olive oil, a jar of pesto, mayonnaise, sun-dried tomatoes and olive paste will enable you to provide a feast, as long as you have some good bread to fill. Remember: you don't have to stick to any particular filling for a certain bread – chop and change to suit your appetite, or what you have available. Once opened, most bottled sauces should be stored in the refrigerator, where they will keep for about a month, but read the labels carefully for advice. Ready-made (as opposed to dry) mustard can be kept in the store-cupboard, but not for too long, as it begins to dry out and darken after a few months.

Dill mustard sauce
This is a sweetened mustard sauce flavoured with dill. It is excellent mixed with a little soured cream and served with gravlax.

Extra-virgin olive oil
This oil is used for flavour in marinades and dressings, and as a dip for bread.

Jalapeño peppers
These are pickled green chillies from Mexico. They are very hot, and are a useful addition to tacos and tostados.

Mustards
Mustards are made from black, brown or white mustard seeds which are ground and then mixed with spices and, usually, wine vinegar. There are many flavoured mustards available, including horseradish, honey, chilli and tarragon. Meaux mustard is made from mixed mustard seed, and has a grainy texture with a warm, spicy flavour. Dijon mustard is medium-hot with a sharp taste, and is ideal in dressings. German mustard has a sweet-sour flavour, and is best with frankfurters.

Olive paste
This is made with puréed black or green olives, olive oil and herbs. Delicious on its own, spread on some good bread, it is also very useful for spreading on bread before covering with topping and grilling (broiling), and for adding to sauces.

Pesto
This is a rich, pungent sauce made with basil, Parmesan cheese, pine nuts and garlic.

Red pesto
This is similar to pesto, but with the addition of sun-dried tomatoes.

Sauerkraut
This salted and fermented white cabbage, often spiced as well, is a useful accompaniment to sausages. It is good mixed with tomato mayonnaise and used in sandwiches.

Sun-dried tomatoes
These are preserved whole by drying and have a dense texture and highly concentrated flavour. You can also buy them chopped and mixed with olive oil and herbs. Delicious used as a spread, or in sauces.

grainy mustard

dill mustard sauce

Dijon mustard

German mustard

black olive paste

pesto

red pesto

crushed sun-dried tomatoes

sun-dried tomatoes

olive oil

chopped chilli

concentrated curry sauce

green olive paste

sauerkraut

Jalapeño peppers

marjoram

coriander

mint

dill

thyme

chives

fennel

nasturtium

violet

rocket (arugula)

basil

flat-leaf parsley

Herbs and Flowers

Fresh herbs have been used liberally in the recipes in this book, for they can give terrific zip to a sandwich filling. They can easily be grown, either in the garden or on a windowsill, and have so much more flavour when they are freshly picked.

Flowers make a delightful garnish, are very pretty to look at and have a sweet taste. Marigolds, pansies, violas, and violets can all be used, as can many of the herb flowers such as borage, thyme, marjoram, mint and rosemary – they all add colour and flavour.

Basil
Basil has a warm, spicy scent and pungent flavour. It is wonderful with tomatoes, and is good used either cooked in a sauce or as fresh leaves added to a sandwich filling.

Chives
Chives give a delicate, mild, onion flavour to sauces and fillings. The slender leaves make attractive garnishes, and the beautiful purple flowers can also be eaten.

Coriander
Coriander is an intensely aromatic herb with a spicy flavour; an essential ingredient in Indian, Chinese and Mexican dishes.

Fennel and Dill
These herbs are both from the same family, with similar feathery leaves, but fennel has a more pronounced aniseed flavour. They are particularly good with fish.

Marjoram and Oregano
These herbs belong to the same family and have similar uses, oregano being a little stronger. They are good in tomato sauces and egg dishes. The flowers make a pretty garnish.

Mint
Mint is used mainly as a garnish, but can also be mixed with soft cheeses or added to grilled (broiled) meats.

Nasturtium
Nasturtium flowers are edible and make a stunning addition to sandwiches. The leaves have a peppery flavour.

Parsley
Curled and flat-leaf parsley are both available, the latter having a stronger flavour. Apart from being an attractive garnish, parsley is also excellent chopped and added to a herb butter.

Rocket (arugula)
Rocket has a peppery, warm flavour which makes it an excellent addition to many fillings.

Thyme
Thyme should be used in cooked dishes for the best flavour.

Breads

There are many interesting types of bread available now – different sizes, shapes, textures, flavours, even colours – making it possible for the sandwich enthusiast to be much more adventurous and to produce some exciting and very tasty creations. Do make the most of the wide variety on offer.

Bagel
Bagels are best served warm, and are especially good when filled with cream cheese and smoked salmon or mackerel pâté

Baguette
Baguettes, or French sticks, can be split lengthways, grilled and cut into lengths to suit the appetite.

Brioche
This light, rich, slightly sweet bread makes a good base for open sandwiches when toasted.

Ciabatta
Ciabatta is made with olive oil and has a light texture. It is available plain or flavoured.

Cottage loaf
A crusty white loaf, suitable for hearty and toasted sandwiches.

Croissant
Croissants are delicious with both sweet and savoury fillings. Warm them first, then split and fill.

Flavoured sticks
These might include granary, onion bread and cheese and herb sticks. They all make excellent vehicles for many fillings.

Pitta bread
These are available in both wholemeal and white, in rounds, ovals and mini cocktail shapes. They are ideal for filling with grilled meats and salads.

Pugliese
This is also known as Italian peasant bread, and is a close-textured loaf made with olive oil.

Pumpernickel
This is a heavy, close-textured black rye bread with a distinctive flavour. It is excellent as a base for open sandwiches, topped with strongly flavoured foods.

Tortilla
This traditional Mexican pancake comes in both corn and wheat varieties. Always warm first before serving with a savoury filling.

Rye bread
Both light and dark rye breads are available. Rye bread is delicious with pickled herring.

Rye with sunflower seeds
This is similar to pumpernickel but lighter in colour and flavour. It is a good base for open sandwiches.

White bread
White bread need not be the pre-packaged, pre-sliced variety. Bakeries will make their own varieties, which have a lot more flavour and a better texture.

Wholemeal (wholewheat) bread
Wholemeal (wholewheat) bread is preferred by some to white bread for its flavour and texture.

croissants

pugliese (Italian peasant bread)

bagels

pumpernickel

ciabatta rolls

ciabatta

baguette

pitta bread

half-baguette

wheat tortillas

brioche

rye breads

rye bread with
sunflower seeds

granary stick

corn tortillas

white loaf

wholemeal (wholewheat) bread

cottage loaf

Cheese and Tomato Stick

A wholesome granary bread with the addition of tomato and Parmesan cheese.

Makes 2 sticks

INGREDIENTS
225 g/8 oz/2 cups wholemeal (whole-wheat) flour
225 g/8 oz/2 cups plain (all-purpose) flour
5 ml/1 tsp salt
5 ml/1 tsp dried yeast
300 ml/10 fl oz/1¼ cups warm water
pinch of sugar
30 ml/2 tbsp tomato purée (paste) or sun-dried tomato paste
25 g/1 oz/¼ cup grated Parmesan cheese
4 spring onions (scallions), chopped
cracked wheat or sesame seeds

1 Mix the flours and salt in a bowl. Put the yeast in a small bowl and mix in half the water and a pinch of sugar to help activate the yeast. Leave for 10 minutes until dissolved, then add to the flour.

2 Add the tomato purée (paste), cheese, spring onions (scallions) and remaining water. Mix to a soft dough, adding a little more water if necessary.

3 Turn out on to a floured surface and knead for 5 minutes until the dough is smooth and elastic.

CHEESE AND TOMATO ROLLS

Divide the dough into 8 portions and shape into rolls. Bake for 20–25 minutes.

GRANARY BREAD

Replace the plain (all-purpose) flour with malted brown flour and omit the last 4 ingredients. Shape the dough into an oblong and place it in a greased 450 g/1 lb loaf tin (bread pan). Bake as above, but allow an extra 5 minutes until the loaf sounds hollow when tapped underneath.

4 Place in a mixing bowl, cover with a damp cloth and leave in a warm place to rise until doubled in size.

5 Turn out on to a floured surface and knead again for a few minutes. Divide the dough in half, shape each portion into a stick 30 cm/12 in long and place diagonally on a greased baking-sheet.

6 Make diagonal cuts down the length of the sticks, brush with water and sprinkle with cracked wheat or sesame seeds. Cover and leave in a warm place to rise for about 30 minutes until doubled in size. Pre-heat the oven to 220°C/425°F/gas mark 7. Bake the bread in the oven for 10 minutes, then lower the temperature to 200°C/400°F/gas mark 6 and bake for a further 15 minutes.

Filling Ingredients

Avocado
Avocado imparts a subtle flavour to sandwiches, and mixes well with Brie or prawns (shrimp).

Blue cheese
This cheese combines particularly well with pears or other fruit.

Brie
Brie should be soft in the centre when used. It is delicious with avocado and tomato.

Capers
The piquant flavour of capers is useful in dressings.

Cucumber
Remove the skin to make these more digestible.

Gruyère or Emmenthal (Swiss) cheese
This is the classic cheese for melting under the grill.

Hens' eggs
Very versatile; use in almost any form with a variety of toppings.

Lemon
Lemon is a tasty addition to fish fillings.

Lettuce
There are so many different varieties available it is worth experimenting with different combinations.

Mozzarella
Mozzarella is another good melting cheese which blends well with sun-dried tomatoes and olive paste.

Olives
These are a particularly good addition to toasted toppings.

Parma ham
This is cured, matured ham, which is sliced very thinly. It is suitable for delicate party sandwiches.

Parmesan
Use freshly grated Parmesan for the best flavour.

Pastrami
Pastrami is cured brisket of beef, which is then smoked. It is best served with a strong-flavoured bread such as rye.

Peppers
These make a crunchy and flavourful addition to fillings.

Prawns (shrimp)
For the best flavour, use North Atlantic prawns (shrimp).

Quails' eggs
A luxurious addition to open sandwiches. Boil for 5 minutes, plunge into cold water and peel.

Rollmop herrings
Rollmops and other varieties of pickled herring are excellent for open sandwiches.

Salami
There is a huge range of salamis available, both smoked and unsmoked.

Smoked salmon
This is ideal for open sandwiches and pinwheels, and can be chopped and served in croissants.

Tomatoes
Again, these come in so many different varieties that it is worth experimenting. Make sure they are deep red for the best flavour.

Gruyère (Swiss) cheese

blue cheese

Brie cheese

mozzarella

Parmesan cheese

rollmop herring

prawns (shrimp)

smoked salmon

pastrami

lemon

tomatoes

avocado

cucumber

lollo rosso lettuce

salami

peppers

quails' eggs

hens' eggs

olives

frisée lettuce

Parma ham

Mayonnaise

Mayonnaise can be made with a small proportion of olive oil to give a fuller flavour, but the result is too rich and heavy if it is made solely with olive oil. It can be made by hand, but may also be successfully prepared in a food processor or blender – whizz 1 whole egg together with the seasonings and vinegar, then gradually add the oil in a thin stream. Store in an airtight container in the refrigerator for up to 2 weeks.

Makes about 350 ml/12 fl oz/1 1/2 cups

INGREDIENTS
2 egg yolks
salt and pepper
2.5 ml/1/2 tsp Dijon mustard
300 ml/10 fl oz/1 1/4 cups sunflower oil
10 ml/2 tsp wine vinegar

1 Beat the egg yolk, seasoning and mustard together in a bowl with a hand whisk. Add the oil drop by drop, whisking vigorously.

2 As the mixture thickens, add the vinegar, then continue to add the remaining oil in a steady stream, whisking all the time. Add a little boiling water to thin if necessary.

Gravlax Sauce

This is used with gravlax, Scandinavian marinated salmon, but its piquant flavour goes well with beef too. It will keep for up to 2 weeks in a sealed container in the refrigerator.

Makes about 150 ml/5 fl oz/2/3 cup

INGREDIENTS
30 ml/2 tbsp German mustard
5 ml/1 tsp caster (superfine) sugar
5 ml/1 tsp wine vinegar
30 ml/2 tbsp oil
30 ml/2 tbsp soured cream
15 ml/1 tbsp chopped fresh dill

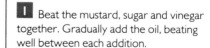

1 Beat the mustard, sugar and vinegar together. Gradually add the oil, beating well between each addition.

2 Mix in the cream and dill.

Peanut Sauce

This peanut sauce is traditionally served with Indonesian satay. It is good with chicken, duck or pork and any vegetable filling, and is also delicious used as a dip. It keeps for up to 1 week in the refrigerator.

Makes about 300 ml/10 fl oz/1¹/₄ cups

INGREDIENTS
15 ml/1 tbsp sunflower oil
1 small onion, chopped
1 garlic clove, crushed
5 ml/1 tsp ground cumin
5 ml/1 tsp ground coriander
2.5 ml/¹/₂ tsp chilli powder
45 ml/3 tbsp crunchy peanut butter
10 ml/2 tsp soy sauce
5 ml/1 tsp lemon juice

1 Heat the oil in a pan and fry the onion until softened. Add the garlic and spices and fry for a further 1 minute, stirring. Mix in the peanut butter and blend in 150 ml/5 fl oz/²/₃ cup water. Bring to the boil, stirring, then cover and cook for 5 minutes.

2 Turn into a bowl and stir in the soy sauce and lemon juice. Thin with a little more water if liked. Allow to cool.

Fennel and Soured Cream Dressing

A light, creamy dressing to use with fish or cucumber fillings. You can make a green herb sauce by adding 45 ml/3 tbsp chopped fresh parsley, chives and mint. It keeps for up to 1 week in the refrigerator.

Makes about 150 ml/5 fl oz/²/₃ cup

INGREDIENTS
100 ml/4 fl oz/¹/₂ cup thick soured
  cream
10 ml/2 tsp lemon juice
1 garlic clove, crushed
5 ml/1 tsp clear honey
30 ml/2 tbsp chopped fresh fennel
salt and pepper

1 Put the soured cream into a bowl, add the lemon juice, garlic and honey and mix thoroughly.

2 Stir in the fennel and some salt and pepper.

Equipment

Very little special equipment is needed for sandwich making, apart from a good bread knife so that you can slice bread evenly and cut sandwiches into portions. Hot sandwich makers, although useful, are by no means essential for making toasted or fried sandwiches – a frying-pan (skillet) or griddle does just as well. However, if you want to make sandwiches for special occasions, or add a little extra flair with garnishes, the following pieces of equipment may be useful to have on hand.

Bread knife
A good-quality bread knife will ensure bread is cut evenly.

Cheese grater
This is invaluable for preparing fillings, both for grating hard cheeses and vegetables.

Cutters
Both plain and shaped cutters are useful for making party sandwiches and canapés. Novelty cutters appeal especially to children.

Knives
Keep knives clean and well sharpened.

Measuring cups
When using measuring cups and spoons make sure you keep to one system of measurement (i.e. metric, imperial or cups).

Measuring spoons
Accurate measuring spoons are essential to successful baking.

Mixing bowls
A set of mixing bowls of various sizes is invaluable. Keep large bowls on hand for making bread (to allow the dough to rise).

Palette knives
Palette knives are useful for spreading fillings smoothly.

Pastry brush
A pastry brush is useful both for bread and sandwich making. Use for egg glazes on uncooked bread dough, and for brushing bread with melted butter or oils.

Rolling pin
When making sandwiches such as Asparagus Rolls, flatten slices of bread with a heavy rolling pin, so that the slices roll up more easily.

Saucepan
A heavy metal saucepan should be used for melted and cooked fillings.

Spatula
Use a flexible spatula for spreading and transferring fillings from mixing bowls.

Spoons, metal
Ordinary soup and dessert spoons may be used for mixing ingredients.

Spoons, wooden
Wooden spoons may be used for mixing both hot and cold fillings.

Wire whisk
Use a wire whisk for mixing hot fillings and sauces.

mixing bowls

cheese grater

bread knife

palette knives

wire whisk

metal spoons

saucepan

cutters

wooden
spoon

pastry brush

measuring jug

rolling pin

knives

measuring spoons

spatula

Avocado Filling

This filling is particularly suitable for sandwich horns, croissants or on open sandwiches.

INGREDIENTS
1 avocado, stoned (pitted) and
    chopped
1 spring onion (scallion), chopped
10 ml/2 tsp lemon juice
dash Worcestershire sauce
salt and pepper

1 Put the avocado pieces in a blender, or mash with a fork until smooth. Mix in the chopped spring onion, lemon juice and seasonings and blend well.

Tuna and Tomato Filling

This recipe is sufficient to fill 3 rounds sandwiches.

INGREDIENTS
75 g/3 oz can tuna fish, drained
25 g/1 oz/2 tbsp softened butter or
    margarine
15 ml/1 tbsp tomato ketchup
15 ml/1 tbsp mayonnaise
salt and pepper

1 Put the tuna fish in a bowl and flake with a fork. Add the butter or margarine, tomato ketchup and mayonnaise and season to taste. Mix well until blended.

Egg and Cress Filling

This recipe is sufficient to fill 3 rounds sandwiches.

INGREDIENTS
2 hard-boiled eggs, shelled and finely
    chopped
50 g/2 oz/¼ cup curd (smooth
    cottage) cheese
30 ml/2 tbsp mayonnaise
salt and pepper
1 carton mustard and cress

1 Mix the ingredients together in a bowl until thoroughly combined and smooth.

Garnishes

The presentation of food is almost as important as the taste. The first contact is by sight, and if the food offered appears attractive and appetizing, the taste buds go into action creating the desire to eat.

These suggestions are for garnishes that not only look good, but also add their own flavour.

Radish rose

Remove the stalk, and with the pointed end of a vegetable knife cut petal shapes round the bottom half of the radish, keeping them joined at the base. Cut a second row of petals in between and above the first row, and continue in this way until you reach the top of the radish. Leave in iced water for about an hour until it opens.

Cucumber butterflies

Cut a 1 cm/½ in length of cucumber and halve lengthways into 2 semi-circles. Cut each into 7 slices, leaving them attached along one edge. Fold every other slice back on itself to form the butterfly.

Carrot curl

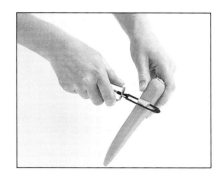

Using a potato peeler remove thin strips of carrot. Roll each strip to make a curl and secure with a cocktail stick (toothpick). Place in iced water for about an hour to keep the shape.

Spring onion (scallion) tassel

Trim a spring onion to about 7.5 cm/3 in long. Cut lengthways through the green part of the onion several times, to within 4 cm/1½ in of the white end. Place in a bowl of iced water for about an hour, until the ends curl up.

Radish chrysanthemum

First remove the stalk, then cut downwards across the radish, using a sharp knife, at 2 mm/1/16 in intervals, keeping the radish joined at the base. Then cut in the opposite direction to form minute squares. Drop into iced water for about an hour, until it opens out like a flower.

Tomato rose

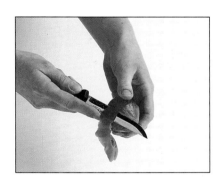

Choose a firm tomato and, starting at the smooth end, pare off the skin in a continuous strip about 1 cm/½ in wide using a sharp knife. With the flesh side inwards, start to curl the strip of skin from the base end, forming a bud shape. Continue winding the strip into a flower.

Filled Croissants

Croissants are very versatile and can be used with sweet or savoury fillings.

Makes 2

INGREDIENTS
2 croissants
knob of butter
2 eggs
salt and pepper
1 tablespoon double (heavy) cream
50 g/2 oz smoked salmon, chopped
1 sprig fresh dill, to garnish

croissants

smoked salmon

eggs

1 Preheat the oven to 180°C/350°F/gas mark 4. Slice the croissants in half horizontally and warm in the oven for 5–6 minutes.

2 Melt a knob of butter in a small pan. Beat the eggs in a bowl with seasoning to taste.

3 Add the eggs to the pan and cook for 2 minutes, stirring constantly.

4 Remove from the heat and stir in the cream and smoked salmon.

5 Spoon the smoked salmon mixture into the warmed croissants and garnish.

Pear and Stilton Filling

Soften 100 g/4 oz Stilton cheese with a fork and mix in 1 peeled, cored and chopped ripe pear and 15 ml/1 tbsp chopped chives with a little black pepper. Spoon into a split croissant and bake in a preheated oven for 5 minutes.

Crispy Hot Dogs

Crisp little envelopes enclose succulent frankfurters –
use grilled (broiled) chipolata sausages if you prefer
and vary the flavouring with different sauces.

Makes 8

INGREDIENTS
8 slices white or brown bread, crusts
    removed
50 g/2 oz/4tbsp soft margarine
15 ml/1 tbsp German mustard
8 frankfurters
sauerkraut, to serve
tomato wedges and flat-leaf parsley,
    to garnish

white bread

frankfurters

mustard

sauerkraut

1 Preheat the oven to 200°C/400°F/gas mark 6. Roll the bread lightly with a rolling pin so that it rolls up more easily.

2 Spread the bread with a little margarine and mustard.

3 Place a frankfurter diagonally across each slice of bread and roll up tightly, securing with a cocktail stick (toothpick). Spread each roll with margarine and place on a baking sheet. Bake in the oven for 15–20 minutes until golden. Meanwhile heat the sauerkraut. Remove the cocktail sticks from the hot dogs and serve with hot sauerkraut and a garnish of tomato wedges and flat-leaf parsley.

Croque Monsieur

Probably the most popular snack food in France, this hot cheese and ham sandwich can be either fried or grilled (broiled).

Makes 2

INGREDIENTS
4 slices white bread
25 g/1 oz/2 tbsp softened butter
2 thin slices lean ham
50 g/2 oz Gruyère (Swiss) cheese,
    thinly sliced
1 sprig flat-leaf parsley, to garnish

white bread

Gruyère (Swiss) chee

ham

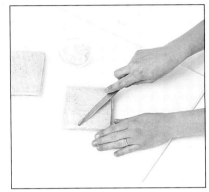

1 Spread the bread with butter.

2 Lay the ham on 2 of the buttered sides of bread.

COOK'S TIP

A flavoured butter can be used to complement a sandwich filling – for example, horseradish butter with beef, mustard butter with ham, lemon and dill butter with fish. To make these just beat the chosen flavouring into the softened butter with some seasoning. Other useful flavourings for butter are: anchovy or curry paste, garlic, herbs, Tabasco or chilli. These butters can also be used in open sandwiches.

3 Lay the Gruyère (Swiss) cheese slices on top of the ham and sandwich with the buttered bread slices. Press firmly together and cut off the crusts.

4 Spread the top with butter, place on a rack and cook for 2½ minutes under the grill (broiler) preheated to a low to moderate temperature.

5 Turn the sandwiches over, spread the remaining butter over the top and return to the grill for a further 2½ minutes until the bread is golden brown and the cheese is beginning to melt. Garnish with a sprig of flat-leaf parsley.

Bruschetta al Pomodoro

Bruschetta is an Italian garlic bread made with the best-quality olive oil you can find and pugliese, a coarse country bread, or ciabatta. Here, chopped tomatoes are added too.

Makes 2

INGREDIENTS
2 large thick slices coarse country
  bread
1 large garlic clove
60 ml/4 tbsp extra-virgin olive oil
2 ripe tomatoes, skinned and chopped
salt and pepper
1 sprig fresh basil, to garnish

country bread

tomatoes

garlic

1 Toast the bread on both sides.

2 Peel the garlic clove and squash with the flat side of a knife blade.

3 Rub the squashed garlic clove over the toast.

4 Drizzle half the olive oil over the toasted bread.

5 Top with the tomatoes, season well and drizzle over the remaining oil. Place under the grill (broiler) to heat through, then garnish with a sprig of basil and eat immediately.

PLAIN BRUSCHETTA
Rub a crushed garlic clove over untoasted bread, drizzle with oil and then toast.

Pastrami on Rye

Pastrami is wood-smoked brisket of beef that has first been dry-cured in a mixture of garlic, sugar, salt and spices. This is a kosher sandwich that originates from New York.

Makes 2

INGREDIENTS

25 g/1 oz/2 tbsp softened butter
4 thin slices rye bread
15 ml/1 tbsp German mustard
100 g/4 oz wafer-thin pastrami
4 gherkins (dill pickles), sliced
    lengthways
radish chrysanthemums and spring
    onion (scallion) tassels, to garnish

rye bread

gherkins (dill pickles)

pastrami

mustard

1 Butter the bread and spread 2 of the slices with a little mustard.

2 Arrange the pastrami slices over the mustard.

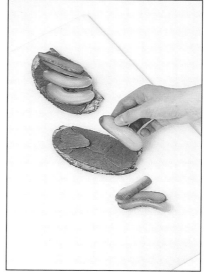

3 Top with slices of gherkin (dill pickle), cover with the remaining bread and press together firmly. Toast on both sides under a preheated grill (broiler) until turning brown. Serve garnished with radish chrysanthemums and spring onion (scallion) tassels.

Fried Mozzarella Sandwich

This sandwich is very popular in southern Italy, where it is known as *Mozzarella in Carrozza*. Do be sure to use the mozzarella packed in brine for the best flavour. This is also excellent made with Cheddar or Gruyère (Swiss) cheese.

Makes 2

INGREDIENTS
100 g/4 oz mozzarella cheese, thickly sliced
4 thick slices white bread, crusts removed
salt and pepper
1 egg
30 ml/2 tbsp milk
oil for shallow-frying

white bread   *mozzarella cheese*

egg

1 Lay the mozzarella slices on 2 slices of bread, sprinkle with salt and pepper, then top with the remaining bread slices to make 2 cheese sandwiches.

2 Mix the egg and milk together, season and place in a large shallow dish.

3 Lay the sandwiches in the egg mixture, turn over so that they are saturated and leave there for a few minutes. Pour enough oil into a frying pan (skillet) to give 1 cm/½ in depth. Heat the oil and fry the sandwich for 3–4 minutes, turning once, until golden brown and crisp. Drain well on kitchen paper.

VARIATION
Add 2 chopped sun-dried tomatoes or some black olive paste to the sandwich before soaking in egg.

Tostadas with Refried Beans

A tostada is a crisp, fried tortilla used as a base on which to pile the topping of your choice – a variation on a sandwich and a very tasty snack popular in Mexico and South America.

Makes 6

INGREDIENTS
30 ml/2 tbsp oil
1 onion, chopped
2 garlic cloves, chopped
2.5 ml/½ tsp chilli powder
425 g/15 oz can borlotti or pinto
  beans, drained
150 ml/5 fl oz/⅔ cup chicken stock
15 ml/1 tbsp tomato purée (paste)
30 ml/2 tbsp chopped fresh coriander
salt and pepper
6 wheat or corn tortillas
45 ml/3 tbsp Tomato Salsa
30 ml/2 tbsp soured cream
50 g/2 oz/½ cup grated Cheddar
  cheese
fresh coriander leaves, to garnish

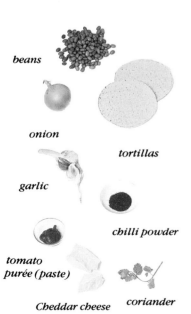

beans

onion

tortillas

garlic

chilli powder

tomato
purée (paste)

Cheddar cheese   coriander

1 Heat the oil in a pan and fry the onion until softened.

2 Add the garlic and chilli powder and fry for 1 minute, stirring.

3 Mix in the beans and mash very roughly with a potato masher.

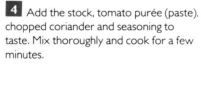

4 Add the stock, tomato purée (paste), chopped coriander and seasoning to taste. Mix thoroughly and cook for a few minutes.

5 Fry the tortillas in hot oil for 1 minute, turning once, until crisp, then drain on kitchen paper.

Tomato Salsa

Makes about 300 ml/10 fl oz/1¼ cups

1 small onion, chopped
1 garlic clove, crushed
2 fresh green chillies, seeded and
   finely chopped, or 5 ml/1 tsp
   bottled chopped chillies
450 g/1 lb tomatoes, skinned and
   chopped
salt
30 ml/2 tbsp chopped fresh coriander

Stir all the ingredients together until
well mixed.

6 Put a spoonful of refried beans on
each tostada, spoon over some Tomato
Salsa, then some soured cream, sprinkle
with grated Cheddar cheese and garnish
with coriander.

Chinese Duck in Pitta

This recipe is based on Chinese crispy duck but uses duck breast instead of whole duck. After 15 minutes' cooking, the duck breast will still have a pinkish tinge. If you like it well cooked, leave it in the oven for a further 5 minutes.

Makes 2

INGREDIENTS
1 duck breast, weighing about 175 g/
  6 oz
3 spring onions (scallions)
7.5 cm/3 in piece cucumber
2 round pitta breads
30 ml/2 tbsp hoi-sin sauce
radish chrysanthemum and spring
  onion (scallion) tassel, to garnish

pitta breads

cucumber

hoi-sin sauce

duck breast

spring onions (scallions)

1 Preheat the oven to 220°C/425°F/gas mark 7. Skin the duck breast, place the skin and breast separately on a rack and cook in the oven for 10 minutes.

2 Remove the skin from the oven, cut into pieces and return to the oven for a further 5 minutes.

3 Meanwhile cut the spring onions (scallions) and cucumber into fine shreds about 4 cm/1 ½ in long.

4 Heat the pitta bread in the oven for a few minutes until puffed up, then split in half to make a pocket.

5 Slice the duck breast thinly.

6 Stuff the duck breast into the pitta bread with a little spring onion, cucumber, crispy duck skin and some hoi-sin sauce. Serve garnished with a radish chrysanthemum and spring onion tassel.

Tuna Melt

Melts can also be made with a variety of meats such as salami, pastrami beef or chicken, then covered with cheese and griddled or grilled (broiled).

Makes 2

INGREDIENTS
90 g/3½ oz can tuna fish, drained and roughly flaked
30 ml/2 tbsp mayonnaise
15 ml/1 tbsp finely chopped celery
15 ml/1 tbsp finely chopped spring onion (scallion)
15 ml/1 tbsp chopped fresh parsley
5 ml/1 tsp lemon juice
25 g/1 oz/2 tbsp softened butter
4 slices wholemeal (wholewheat) bread
50 g/2 oz Gruyère or Emmenthal (Swiss) cheese, sliced
celery leaves and radish roses, to garnish

wholemeal (wholewheat) bread

celery

spring onion (scallion)

tuna fish

Gruyère (Swiss) cheese

parsley

1 Mix together the tuna fish, mayonnaise, celery, spring onion (scallion), parsley and lemon juice.

2 Butter the bread slices with half the butter and spread the tuna filling over 2 of them. Cover with the cheese slices, then sandwich with the remaining bread.

3 Butter the bread on top and place under a moderate grill (broiler) for 1–2 minutes. Turn over, spread with the remaining butter and grill for a further 1–2 minutes until the cheese begins to melt. Garnish with celery leaves and radish roses.

PASTRAMI MELT

Arrange 2 slices pastrami over a slice of rye bread and spread some mustard on top. Cover with tomato and onion slices, then top with cheese, cover with the buttered bread and griddle or grill (broil) on both sides.

Reuben Sandwich

A popular American sandwich, a New York Jewish creation, that combines rye bread or pumpernickel, salt beef, Gruyère (Swiss) cheese and sauerkraut. The grilled (broiled) sandwich should be crisp and hot outside and cold inside.

Makes 2

INGREDIENTS

25 g/1 oz/2 tbsp softened butter
4 slices rye bread or pumpernickel
50 g/2 oz wafer-thin salt beef
50 g/2 oz Gruyère or Emmenthal
    (Swiss) cheese, sliced
15 ml/1 tbsp tomato ketchup
30 ml/2 tbsp mayonnaise
90 ml/6 tbsp sauerkraut
sliced gherkins (dill pickles) and
    celery leaves, to garnish

rye bread

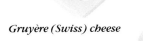
Gruyère (Swiss) cheese

sauerkraut

salt beef

1 Butter the pumpernickel and place salt beef on 2 of the slices. Arrange cheese on the other slices.

2 Mix the tomato ketchup and mayonnaise with the sauerkraut.

3 Pile the sauerkraut mixture on top of the cheese and spread to the edges.

4 Lay the other slices, beef side down, on top of the sauerkraut. Butter the bread on top, then grill (broil) for 1–2 minutes until crisp. Turn over, butter the second side and grill for a further 1–2 minutes until the cheese just begins to melt. Serve garnished with gherkin (dill pickle) slices and celery leaves.

VARIATION
Replace the salt beef with pastrami.

Reuben Sandwich

A popular American sandwich, a New York Jewish creation, that combines rye bread or pumpernickel, salt beef, Gruyère (Swiss) cheese and sauerkraut. The grilled (broiled) sandwich should be crisp and hot outside and cold inside.

Makes 2

INGREDIENTS
25 g/1 oz/2 tbsp softened butter
4 slices rye bread or pumpernickel
50 g/2 oz wafer-thin salt beef
50 g/2 oz Gruyère or Emmenthal
   (Swiss) cheese, sliced
15 ml/1 tbsp tomato ketchup
30 ml/2 tbsp mayonnaise
90 ml/6 tbsp sauerkraut
sliced gherkins (dill pickles) and
   celery leaves, to garnish

rye bread

Gruyère (Swiss) cheese

sauerkraut

salt beef

1 Butter the pumpernickel and place salt beef on 2 of the slices. Arrange cheese on the other slices.

2 Mix the tomato ketchup and mayonnaise with the sauerkraut.

3 Pile the sauerkraut mixture on top of the cheese and spread to the edges.

4 Lay the other slices, beef side down, on top of the sauerkraut. Butter the bread on top, then grill (broil) for 1–2 minutes until crisp. Turn over, butter the second side and grill for a further 1–2 minutes until the cheese just begins to melt. Serve garnished with gherkin (dill pickle) slices and celery leaves.

VARIATION
Replace the salt beef with pastrami.

Köfte in Pitta Pockets

Köfte is the Turkish name for meatballs. These are
made with minced (ground) lamb and flavoured with
cumin. Pitta bread is also good filled with grilled
(broiled) lamb fillet which has been marinated in a
little wine and olive oil flavoured with garlic, bay
and cumin.

Makes 4

INGREDIENTS
1 slice bread
225 g/8 oz minced (ground) lamb
1 garlic clove, crushed
1 small onion, finely chopped
5 ml/1 tsp ground cumin
15 ml/1 tbsp chopped fresh mint
salt and pepper
15 ml/1 tbsp pine nuts
flour for coating
oil for shallow-frying
4 pitta breads
1 onion, cut into thin rings
2 tomatoes, sliced or cut into wedges

minced (ground) lamb

onion

cumin

bread

mint

pine nuts

garlic

1 Preheat the oven to 220°C/425°F/gas
mark 7. Soak the bread in water for 5
minutes. then squeeze dry and add to
the next 7 ingredients. Mix until
thoroughly blended and malleable. Shape
into small balls the size of a walnut, using
dampened hands so that the mixture
does not stick. Coat in flour.

2 Shallow-fry for about 6 minutes,
turning frequently, until golden brown.

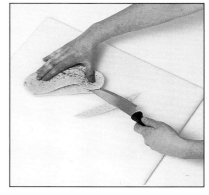

3 Heat the pitta bread in the oven for a
few minutes until puffed up, then cut a
thin strip off one side of each pitta to
make a pocket.

4 Fill with onion rings, tomato wedges
and a few Köfte.

TZATZIKI

Mix together 100 g/4 oz/1½ cups Greek (plain) yogurt, 50 g/2 oz/⅓ cup peeled and grated cucumber, 1 crushed garlic clove, 15 ml/1 tbsp chopped fresh mint and seasoning to taste.

LAMB IN PITTA POCKETS

Mix together 50 ml/2 fl oz/¼ cup red wine, 50 ml/2 fl oz/¼ cup olive oil, 2 chopped garlic cloves, 1 bay leaf and ½ teaspoon each of ground cumin and ground coriander. Marinade a 175 g/6 oz lamb fillet in this mixture for at least 30 minutes. Grill (broil) for 10 minutes, turning once, then slice thinly and stuff into a warmed pitta pocket with salad and Tzatziki.

Chilli Beef Tacos

A taco is a soft wheat or corn tortilla wrapped around a spicy warm savoury filling – you could describe it as a Mexican sandwich.

Makes 4

INGREDIENTS
15 ml/1 tbsp oil
1 small onion, chopped
2 garlic cloves, chopped
175 g/6 oz/¾ cup minced (ground) beef
7 ml/½ tbsp flour
200 g/7 oz can tomatoes
7 ml/½ tbsp Jalapeño peppers, finely chopped
salt
4 wheat or corn tortillas
45 ml/3 tbsp soured cream
½ avocado, peeled, stoned (pitted) and sliced
1 tomato, sliced
Tomato Salsa, to serve (optional)

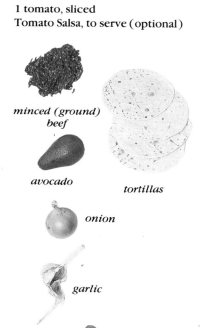

minced (ground) beef

avocado

tortillas

onion

garlic

Jalapeño peppers

1 Heat the oil in a frying-pan (skillet), add the onion and fry until softened. Add the garlic and beef and cook, stirring so that the meat is broken up as it seals.

2 Stir in the flour, then add the canned tomatoes, peppers and salt to taste.

3 Heat the tortillas one at a time in a medium-hot lightly oiled pan.

4 Spread a spoonful of the meat mixture over each tortilla.

5 Top each tortilla with some soured cream and avocado and tomato slices. Roll up and eat immediately with Tomato Salsa if liked.

TOASTED TOPPINGS

Toasted Pizza-topped Scones

Use whatever cheese you have to hand – Cheddar, mozzarella or goat's cheese will all work well. Add a few olives too, if you like.

Makes 12

INGREDIENTS
6 Cheese and Herb Scones
90 ml/6 tbsp red pesto
2 tomatoes, sliced
5 ml/1 tsp dried oregano
salt and pepper
225 g/8 oz/2 cups grated Cheddar
cheese

Cheese and Herb Scones

tomato

Cheddar cheese

oregano

red pesto

1 Cut the scones in half, toast on the cut side and spread with red pesto.

2 Put a slice of tomato on each one and sprinkle with the oregano and seasoning to taste.

3 Pile grated cheese on top of each one and place under a moderate grill (broiler) until brown and bubbling.

CHEESE AND HERB SCONES

These scones are so quick to make, and when cut in half make tasty bases for grilled (broiled) toppings.

Makes 6

225 g/8 oz/2 cups self-raising (self-rising) flour
5 ml/1 tsp mustard powder
cayenne pepper
2.5 ml/½ tsp salt
50 g/2 oz/4 tbsp margarine
5 ml/1 tsp dried oregano
75 g/3 oz/¾ cup grated Cheddar
cheese
100 ml/4 fl oz/½ cup milk, plus extra
to glaze

Preheat the oven to 220°C/425°F/gas mark 7. Sift the flour, mustard, cayenne and salt into a mixing bowl and rub in the margarine until the mixture resembles breadcrumbs. Mix in the oregano and cheese, then add the milk and mix to a soft dough. Turn on to a floured surface, knead and roll out to a thickness of 1 cm/½ in. Cut into 7.5 cm/3 in rounds with a plain cutter, place on a floured baking sheet and brush with milk. Bake in the oven for 12–15 minutes until golden. Cool on a wire rack.

Ciabatta Rolls with Goat's Cheese

The Tomato Relish gives a piquant bite that nicely complements the goat's cheese. If you can't find ciabatta rolls, use a ciabatta loaf instead.

Makes 4

INGREDIENTS
2 ciabatta rolls
60 ml/4 tbsp Tomato Relish
30 ml/2 tbsp chopped fresh basil
175 g/6 oz goat's cheese, thinly sliced
6 black olives, halved and stoned (pitted)
1 sprig fresh basil, to garnish

ciabatta rolls

Tomato Relish

goat's cheese

basil

olives

1 Cut the rolls in half and toast on one side only.

2 Spread a little relish over each half and sprinkle with the chopped basil.

3 Arrange the goat's cheese slices on this and scatter a few olives over the top. Place under a hot grill (broiler) until the goat's cheese begins to melt, then serve garnished with a sprig of basil.

TOMATO RELISH

Makes 450 ml/15 fl oz/scant 2 cups

45 ml/3 tbsp olive oil
1 onion, chopped
1 red (bell) pepper, seeded and chopped
2 garlic cloves
¼ tsp chilli powder
400 g/14 oz can chopped tomatoes
15 ml/1 tbsp clear honey
10 ml/2 tsp black olive paste
30 ml/2 tbsp red wine vinegar
salt and pepper

Heat the oil and fry the onion and red (bell) pepper until softened. Add the garlic and the remaining ingredients, and season to taste. Simmer for 15 minutes until thickened.

Ciabatta with Mozzarella and Grilled Onion

Ciabatta is readily available in most supermarkets. It's even more delicious when made with spinach, sun-dried tomatoes or olives, and you'll probably find these in your local delicatessen.

Makes 4

INGREDIENTS
1 ciabatta loaf
60 ml/4 tbsp red pesto
2 small onions
oil, for brushing
225 g/8 oz mozzarella cheese
8 black olives

ciabatta loaf

tomato

onion

mozzarella

olives

red pesto

1 Cut the bread in half horizontally and toast lightly. Spread with the red pesto.

2 Peel the onions and cut horizontally into thick slices. Brush with oil and grill (broil) for 3 minutes until lightly browned.

3 Slice the cheese and arrange over the bread. Lay the onion slices on top and scatter some olives over. Cut in half diagonally. Place under a hot grill for 2–3 minutes until the cheese melts and the onion chars.

Welsh Rarebit

This recipe is traditionally made with brown ale (beer) or red wine, which gives it a delicious flavour. You can use other cheeses too, such as Stilton or Red Leicester. If you put a poached or fried egg on top, the dish becomes a Buck Rarebit.

Makes 4

INGREDIENTS
100 g/4 oz/1 cup grated strong
    Cheddar cheese
30 ml/2 tbsp brown ale (beer)
5 ml/1 tsp English mustard
cayenne pepper
4 slices bread

bread

brown ale (beer)

mustard

Cheddar cheese

cayenne pepper

1 Put the cheese in a saucepan with the brown ale (beer), mustard and cayenne pepper and mix together thoroughly.

2 Heat gently, stirring constantly, until the cheese is just beginning to melt.

3 Meanwhile toast the bread. Spread the cheese mixture over the toast.

4 Grill (broil) lightly until tinged brown here and there.

Crostini with Tomato and Anchovy

Crostini are little rounds of bread cut from a French stick and toasted or fried, then covered with a savoury topping such as melted cheese, olive paste, anchovy, tomato or chicken liver.

Makes 8

INGREDIENTS
1 small French stick (large enough to give 8 slices)
30 ml/2 tbsp olive oil
2 garlic cloves, chopped
4 tomatoes, skinned and chopped
15 ml/1 tbsp chopped fresh basil
15 ml/1 tbsp tomato purée (paste)
salt and pepper
8 canned anchovy fillets
12 black olives, halved and stoned (pitted)
1 sprig fresh basil, to garnish

olive oil

French stick

garlic

black olives

basil

anchovy fillets

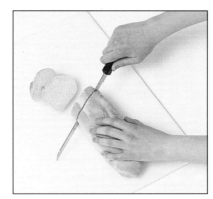

I Cut the loaf diagonally into 8 slices about 1 cm/½ in thick and toast until golden on both sides.

CROSTINI WITH ONION AND OLIVE

Fry 350 g/12 oz/2 cups sliced onions in 30 ml/2 tbsp olive oil till golden brown. Stir in 8 roughly chopped anchovy fillets, 12 halved, stoned (pitted) black olives, some seasoning and 5 ml/1 tsp dried thyme. Spread the toasted bread with 15 ml/1 tbsp black olive paste and spread a spoonful of the onion mixture over each one.

2 Heat the oil and fry the garlic and tomatoes for 4 minutes. Stir in the basil, tomato paste and seasoning.

3 Spoon a little tomato mixture on to each slice of bread. Place an anchovy fillet on each one and sprinkle with olives. Serve garnished with a sprig of basil.

Focaccia with Hot Artichokes and Olives

Focaccia makes an excellent base for different grilled (broiled) toppings. Artichoke hearts bottled in oil are best for this.

Makes 3

INGREDIENTS
60 ml/4 tbsp olive paste
3 Mini Focaccia
1 small red (bell) pepper, halved and seeded
275 g/10 oz bottled or canned artichoke hearts, drained
75 g/3 oz pepperoni, sliced
5 ml/1 tsp dried oregano

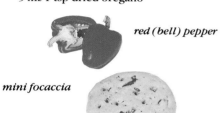

red (bell) pepper

mini focaccia

oregano

pepperoni

artichoke hearts

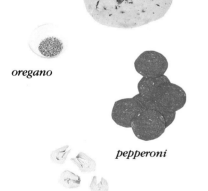

1 Preheat the oven to 220°C/425°F/gas mark 7. Spread the olive paste over the focaccia. Grill (broil) the red pepper till blackened, put in a plastic bag, seal and allow to cool for 10 minutes. Skin the pepper and cut into strips.

2 Cut the artichoke hearts in quarters and arrange over the paste with the pepperoni.

3 Sprinkle over the red pepper strips and the oregano. Place in the oven for 5–10 minutes until heated through.

OLIVE FOCACCIA

Focaccia is an Italian flat bread made with olive oil and often with olives as well. The amount of water needed varies with the type of flour used, so you may need a little less – or a little more – than the given quantity.

Makes 2 loaves

450 g/1 lb/4 cups strong white (bread) flour
5 ml/1 tsp salt
5 ml/1 tsp dried yeast
pinch of sugar
300 ml/10 fl oz/1¼ cups warm water
60 ml/4 tbsp olive oil
100 g/4 oz/1 cup black olives, stoned (pitted) and roughly chopped
2.5 ml/½ tsp dried oregano

Mix the flour and salt together in a mixing bowl. Put the yeast in a small bowl and mix with half the water and a pinch of sugar to help activate the yeast. Leave for about 10 minutes until dissolved. Add the yeast mixture to the flour along with the oil, olives and remaining water and mix to a soft dough, adding a little more water if necessary.

Turn the dough out on to a floured surface and knead for 5 minutes until it is smooth and elastic. Place in a mixing bowl, cover with a damp tea (dish) towel and leave in a warm place to rise for about 2 hours or until doubled in size.

Preheat the oven to 220°C/425°F/ gas mark 7. Turn the dough out on to a floured surface and knead again for a few minutes. Divide into 2 portions, then roll out each to a thickness of 1 cm/½ in in either a round or oblong shape. Place on an oiled baking sheet using a floured rolling pin to lift the dough. Make indentations all over the surface using your fingertips and sprinkle with the oregano. Bake in the oven for about 15–20 minutes.

FOCACCIA WITH MOZZARELLA AND SUN-DRIED TOMATOES

Spread the focaccia with 45 ml/3 tbsp chopped sun-dried tomatoes. Slice 225 g/8 oz mozzarella cheese and arrange over the top. Sprinkle with 8 stoned (pitted) and quartered black olives, and heat through in the oven as for the main recipe.

MINI FOCACCIA

Divide the dough into 6 balls. On a floured surface roll these out to 15 cm/6 in circles. Finish as for Olive Focaccia, baking for 12–15 minutes.

Pan Bagna

This literally means 'bathed bread' and is basically a
Salade Niçoise stuffed into a baguette or roll. The olive
oil dressing soaks into the bread when it is left for an
hour or so with a weight on top of it.

Makes 4

INGREDIENTS
1 large baguette
150 ml/5 fl oz/⅔ cup French Dressing
1 small onion, thinly sliced
3 tomatoes, sliced
1 small green or red (bell) pepper,
    seeded and sliced
50 g/2 oz can anchovy fillets, drained
90 g/3½ oz can tuna fish, drained
50 g/2 oz black olives, halved and
    stoned (pitted)

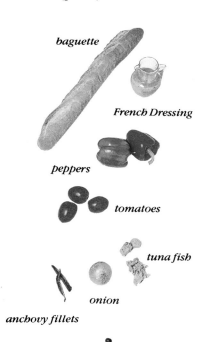

baguette

French Dressing

peppers

tomatoes

tuna fish

onion

anchovy fillets

olives

1 Split the baguette horizontally along
one side without cutting all the way
through the crust.

2 Open the bread out so that it lies flat
and sprinkle the French Dressing evenly
over the top.

3 Arrange the onion, tomatoes, green
or red pepper, anchovies, tuna and olives
on one side of the bread. Close the 2
halves, pressing firmly together.

4 Wrap in clear film (plastic wrap), lay a
board on top, put a weight on it and leave
for about 1 hour: as well as allowing the
dressing to soak into the bread, this
makes it easier to eat.

5 Cut the loaf diagonally into 4 equal
portions.

FRENCH DRESSING

Olive oil is a must for this dressing; it
imparts a rich, fruity flavour,
especially if you use that lovely green,
virgin olive oil. Make a large quantity
at a time and store it in a wine bottle,
ready for instant use.

Makes about 450 ml/¾ pint/scant 2
cups

350 ml/12 fl oz/1½ cups extra-virgin
    olive oil
90 ml/6 tbsp red wine vinegar
15 ml/1 tbsp Moutarde de Meaux
1 garlic clove, crushed
5 ml/1 tsp clear honey
salt and pepper

Pour the olive oil into a measuring jug
and make up to 450 ml/¾ pint/scant 2
cups with the vinegar. Add the
remaining ingredients, then, using a
funnel pour into a wine bottle. Put in
the cork firmly, give the mixture a
thorough shake and store.

Ciabatta Sandwich

If you can find a ciabatta flavoured with sun-dried tomatoes, it improves the flavour of the sandwich. Parma ham should be very thinly sliced and then cut into strips to make it easier to eat.

Makes 3

INGREDIENTS
60 ml/4 tbsp mayonnaise
30 ml/2 tbsp pesto
1 ciabatta loaf
100 g/4 oz provolone or mozzarella cheese, sliced
75 g/3 oz Parma ham, cut into strips
4 plum tomatoes, sliced
sprigs fresh basil, torn into pieces

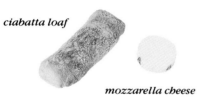

ciabatta loaf

mozzarella cheese

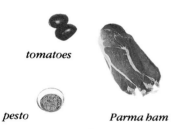

tomatoes

pesto

Parma ham

basil

1 Thoroughly mix together the mayonnaise and pesto sauce.

2 Cut the ciabatta in half horizontally and spread the cut side of both halves with the pesto mayonnaise. Lay the cheese over one half of the ciabatta.

3 Cut the Parma ham into strips and arrange over the top. Cover with the sliced tomatoes and torn basil leaves. Sandwich together with the other half and cut into 3 pieces.

Frankfurter and Potato Salad Sandwich

An unlikely mixture to put into a sandwich, but one that works extremely well. If the potato salad is a bit too chunky, chop it a little first. This is best eaten with a knife and fork.

Makes 2

INGREDIENTS
100 g/4 oz/²⁄₃ cup potato salad
2 spring onions (scallions), chopped
25 g/1 oz/2 tbsp softened butter
4 slices wholemeal (wholewheat)
　bread
4 frankfurters
2 tomatoes, sliced

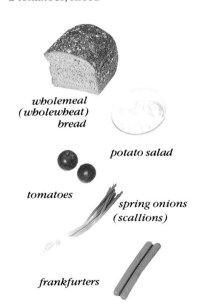

*wholemeal
(wholewheat)
bread*

potato salad

tomatoes

*spring onions
(scallions)*

frankfurters

FRANKFURTER AND EGG FILLING

Shell and roughly chop 1 hard-boiled egg and mix with 15 ml/1 tbsp mayonnaise and 15 ml/1 tbsp chopped fresh chives. Use in place of the potato salad.

1 Mix the potato salad with the spring onions (scallions).

2 Butter all 4 slices of bread and divide the potato salad equally between 2 of them, spreading it to the edges.

3 Slice the frankfurters diagonally and arrange over the potato salad with the tomato slices.

4 Sandwich with the remaining bread, press together lightly and cut in half.

Omelette Roll

An unusual way to serve an omelette but one that works extremely well eaten either warm or cold. It's equally good made with wholemeal (wholewheat) bread, in which case don't roll the omelette.

Makes 1

INGREDIENTS
1 Cheese and Tomato Roll
10 ml/2 tsp crushed sun-dried tomatoes
2 eggs
salt and pepper
few sprigs watercress
30 ml/2 tbsp chopped fresh chives
15 ml/1 tbsp chopped sun-dried tomatoes
15 g/½ oz/1 tbsp butter

Cheese and Tomato Roll

chives

eggs

sun-dried tomatoes

crushed sun-dried tomatoes

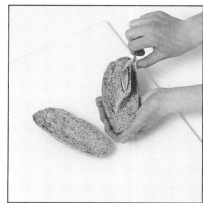

1 Slice the roll horizontally, scoop out some of the crumb to make a hollow, and spread the crushed sun-dried tomato over the bread.

2 Break the eggs into a small bowl, add seasoning, 15 ml/1 tbsp water, the watercress, chives, and chopped sun-dried tomato and whisk with a fork.

3 Heat the butter in a small omelette pan until it sizzles.

4 Tip in the egg, then, as it begins to set, draw the sides towards the middle, so that more egg touches the hot pan. Repeat this a couple more times.

5 When the egg is just set, lift the edge of the omelette nearest the handle, tilting the pan away from you.

6 Flip the omelette over and gently slip it into the roll.

Salami Hero

This is a huge affair, filled with as much as you can cram into a roll. This American speciality varies regionally, and can contain tuna, egg, cheese, coleslaw, salads, meats or salamis according to your taste, or whatever is available.

Makes 2

INGREDIENTS
2 long crusty rolls
25 g/1 oz/2 tbsp softened butter
few leaves lollo rosso lettuce or
    radicchio
75 g/3 oz coleslaw
75 g/3 oz Italian salami, sliced
1 tomato, sliced
30 ml/2 tbsp mayonnaise

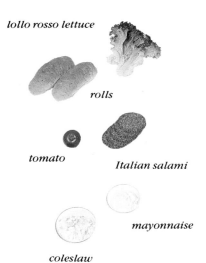

lollo rosso lettuce

rolls

tomato

Italian salami

mayonnaise

coleslaw

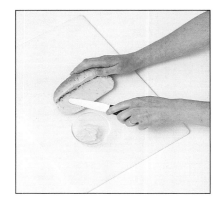

1 Cut the rolls horizontally three-quarters of the way through, open out sufficiently to take the filling and butter both cut sides.

2 Arrange lettuce or radicchio leaves on the base, then add a spoonful of coleslaw.

3 Fold the salami slices in half and arrange over the top. Cover with a little more lettuce, tomato slices and a little mayonnaise. Serve with a napkin!

Classic BLT

This delicious American sandwich is made with crispy fried bacon, lettuce and tomato. Choose the bread you prefer and toast it if you like.

Makes 2

INGREDIENTS
4 slices granary bread
15 g/½ oz/1 tbsp softened butter
few crisp lettuce leaves, cos or
   iceberg
1 large tomato, sliced
8 rashers (slices) streaky bacon
30 ml/2 tbsp mayonnaise

granary bread

tomato

lettuce

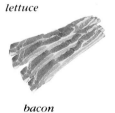

bacon

1 Spread 2 of the slices of bread with butter. Lay the lettuce over the bread and cover with sliced tomato.

2 Grill (broil) the bacon until it begins to crisp, then arrange it over the sliced tomato.

3 Spread the 2 remaining slices of bread with mayonnaise. Lay over the bacon, press the sandwich together gently and cut in half.

Club Sandwich

Club sandwiches, or triple-deckers, are made with 3 layers of bread and should be very generously filled. The filling can be varied – chicken, ham, cheese or beef, with a relish to complement and then a layer of salad and, of course, mayonnaise.

Makes 1

INGREDIENTS
25 g/1 oz/2 tbsp softened butter
2 slices brown bread
1 slice white bread
2 slices rare roast beef
5 ml/1 tsp Horseradish Relish
few leaves curly endive
1 tomato, sliced
½ avocado, peeled and sliced
30 ml/2 tbsp mayonnaise
carrot curls and stuffed olives, to
    garnish

bread

tomato

avocado

endive

roast beef

mayonnaise

1 Butter the brown bread on one side only and the white bread on both sides.

2 Cover one of the brown slices with 2 slices beef, some Horseradish Relish and then some curly endive.

3 Cover this layer with the white bread and then arrange tomato and avocado slices on top.

4 Spread mayonnaise over the top, and sandwich with the remaining brown slice of bread.

5 Press together lightly and cut into quarters.

HORSERADISH RELISH

Makes about 75 ml/3 fl oz/⅓ cup

45 ml/3 tbsp fromage frais
20 ml/4 tsp grainy mustard
20 ml/4 tsp horseradish sauce

Mix all ingredients together in a bowl.

6 Put carrot curls and stuffed olives on cocktail sticks (toothpicks) and stick into each sandwich to garnish.

Prawn, Tomato and Mayonnaise Sandwich

Use frozen North Atlantic prawns (shrimp) for the best flavour, and make quite sure that they are thoroughly defrosted and well drained before you assemble the sandwich. Pat them dry with kitchen paper.

Makes 2

INGREDIENTS
25 g/1 oz/2 tbsp softened butter
5 ml/1 tsp sun-dried tomato paste
4 slices wholemeal (wholewheat)
   bread
1 bunch watercress, trimmed
45 ml/3 tbsp Tomato Mayonnaise
100 g/4 oz/⅔ cup frozen cooked
   peeled prawns (shrimp), defrosted

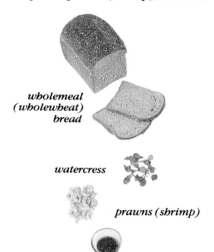

*wholemeal
(wholewheat)
bread*

watercress

prawns (shrimp)

sun-dried tomato paste

1 Mix the butter and tomato paste together until well blended.

2 Spread on the bread and then arrange sprigs of watercress on 2 of the slices.

3 Spread Tomato Mayonnaise to the edges, then divide the prawns (shrimp) equally over the top. Sandwich together with the remaining bread slices and cut in half or quarters.

TOMATO MAYONNAISE

Makes 175 ml/6 fl oz/¾ cup

Skin, seed and chop 1 tomato and place in a blender with 1 small crushed garlic clove, 1 tsp soft brown sugar and 10 ml/2 tsp tomato purée (paste). Blend and stir into 100 ml/4 fl oz/½ cup mayonnaise

Chicken and Curry Mayonnaise Sandwich

A very useful and appetizing way of using leftover pieces of chicken.

Makes 2

INGREDIENTS
4 slices granary bread
25 g/1 oz/2 tbsp softened butter
100 g/4 oz/1 cup cooked chicken, sliced
45 ml/3 tbsp Curry Mayonnaise
1 bunch watercress, trimmed

chicken

granary bread

Curry Mayonnaise

watercress

1 Spread the bread with butter and arrange the chicken over 2 of the slices.

2 Spread Curry Mayonnaise over the chicken slices.

3 Arrange sprigs of watercress on top, cover with the remaining bread, press lightly together and cut in half.

CURRY MAYONNAISE

Makes about 150 ml/5 fl oz/⅔ cup

100 ml/4 fl oz/½ cup mayonnaise
10 ml/2 tsp concentrated curry sauce
2.5 ml/½ tsp lemon juice
10 ml/2 tsp sieved (strained) apricot jam

Mix all the ingredients together thoroughly.

Crab and Avocado Sandwich

The flavours of crab and avocado combine together very successfully to make this a most delicious sandwich.

Makes 4

INGREDIENTS
175 g/6 oz canned crab meat in brine, drained
2 spring onions (scallions), chopped
salt and pepper
100 ml/4 fl oz/½ cup mayonnaise
1 large avocado, peeled and halved
15 ml/1 tbsp lemon juice
50 g/2 oz/4 tbsp softened butter
8 slices granary bread
endive leaves, to garnish

mayonnaise

granary bread

avocado

spring onions (scallions)

crab meat

1 Mix the crab meat with the spring onions (scallions), seasoning and 30 ml/2 tbsp of the mayonnaise.

2 Cut the avocado into slices and brush with lemon juice.

3 Butter the bread and divide the crab meat between 4 of the slices, spreading it to the edges.

4 Cover with slices of avocado.

5 Spread the remaining mayonnaise over the top. Cover with the remaining bread slices and press together firmly. Cut off the crusts and cut the sandwiches diagonally into quarters. Garnish with endive leaves.

Oriental Chicken Sandwich

This filling is also good served in warmed pitta bread, in which case cut the chicken into small cubes before marinating, grill (broil) on skewers and serve warm.

Makes 2

INGREDIENTS
15 ml/1 tbsp soy sauce
5 ml/1 tsp clear honey
5 ml/1 tsp sesame oil
1 garlic clove, crushed
175 g/6 oz skinless boneless chicken breast
4 slices white bread
60 ml/4 tbsp Peanut Sauce
25 g/1 oz/¼ cup beansprouts
25 g/1 oz/¼ cup red (bell) pepper, seeded and finely sliced
2 sprigs parsley, to garnish

chicken breast

garlic

beansprouts

pepper

Peanut Sauce

1 Mix together the soy sauce, honey, sesame oil and garlic. Brush over the chicken breast.

2 Grill (broil) the chicken for 3–4 minutes on each side until cooked through, then slice thinly.

3 Spread 2 slices of the bread with some of the Peanut Sauce.

4 Lay the chicken on the sauce-covered bread.

5 Spread a little more sauce over the chicken.

6 Sprinkle over the beansprouts and red (bell) pepper and sandwich together with the remaining slices of bread.

Tuna and Sweetcorn Bap

Tuna and sweetcorn make a delicious combination.
It's a rather soft filling, so it is better served in a roll,
which is firmer to hold, than between slices of bread.

Makes 2

INGREDIENTS
90 g/3½ oz canned tuna fish, drained
  and flaked
90 ml/6 tbsp cooked sweetcorn
  kernels
60 ml/4 tbsp chopped cucumber
2 spring onions (scallions), chopped
90 ml/6 tbsp Tartare Sauce
2 granary baps (rolls)
2 green or lollo rosso lettuce leaves

sweetcorn kernels

lettuce leaves

granary bap (roll)

tuna fish

spring onions (scallions)

Tartare Sauce

cucumber

1 Mix together the tuna fish,
sweetcorn, cucumber, spring onions and
30 ml/2 tbsp of the Tartare Sauce.

2 Cut the baps in half and divide the
filling between each bottom half.

TARTARE SAUCE
Mix together 90 ml/6 tbsp
mayonnaise with 10 ml/2 tsp each of
chopped gherkins (dill pickle),
chopped capers and chopped parsley.

3 Place a lettuce leaf on top, cover with
the remaining Tartare Sauce and replace
the top of each bap.

Bagels and Lox

Bagels were introduced from Germany into the United States with the first Jewish immigrants, but are now popular everywhere. They should be served warm, and the traditional filling is smoked salmon and cream cheese, but other fillings also work well, particularly smoked mackerel.

Makes 2

INGREDIENTS
2 bagels
100 g/4 oz/½ cup cream cheese
5 ml/1 tsp lemon juice
15 ml/1 tbsp chopped fresh chives
salt and pepper
a little milk (optional)
100 g/4 oz smoked salmon
dill sprigs and lemon slices, to garnish

bagels

smoked salmon

chives

cream cheese

1 Preheat the oven to 180°C/350°F/gas mark 4. Wrap the bagels in foil and warm through in the oven for 10 minutes. Mix the cream cheese with the lemon juice, chives, seasoning and a little milk to thin if necessary.

2 Cut the bagels in half horizontally and spread the bases with the cream cheese.

3 Arrange the smoked salmon over the cream cheese and replace the tops of the bagels.

Farmer's Brunch

A new and tasty twist to a traditional, wholesome sandwich. Use very fresh crusty white bread and top the cheese with a home-made Peach Relish, which goes particularly well with Red Leicester cheese.

Makes 2

INGREDIENTS
4 slices crusty white bread
25 g/1 oz/2 tbsp softened butter
100 g/4 oz Red Leicester or
    Wensleydale cheese (Monterey Jack
    or Tilamook), sliced
45 ml/3 tbsp Peach Relish
spring onions (scallions), or pickled
    onions, and tomato wedges, to serve

white bread

Red Leicester

tomato

spring onion (scallion)

Peach Relish

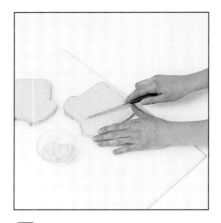

1 Butter the bread.

2 Cover 2 slices with cheese.

3 Spread Peach Relish over the remaining 2 slices and place them over the cheese.

4 Cut in half and serve with spring onions or pickled onions, and tomato wedges.

PEACH RELISH

A very quick relish that can be eaten immediately. It will keep up to 1 month in the refrigerator.

Makes about 700 ml/25 fl oz/3 cups relish

60 ml/4 tbsp wine vinegar
60 ml/4 tbsp light soft brown sugar
5 ml/1 tsp finely chopped chilli
5 ml/1 tsp finely chopped ginger
5 peaches, stoned (pitted) and
    chopped
1 yellow (bell) pepper, seeded and
    chopped
1 small onion, chopped

Put the vinegar and sugar in a saucepan with the chilli and ginger and heat gently until the sugar has dissolved.

Add the remaining ingredients and bring to the boil, stirring constantly.

Cover and cook gently for 15 minutes. Remove the lid and cook for a further 10–15 minutes until tender and the liquid is slightly reduced. Pour into warm, clean jars and cover.

Baguette with Pâté

A lovely picnic sandwich, especially good for holidays in France. Fill with pork or duck rillettes, a rich mixture of shredded meat, or a pâté of your choice. It is also delicious filled with Brie or Camembert cheese.

Makes 2

INGREDIENTS
2 demi-baguettes
25 g/1 oz/2 tbsp softened butter
2 tomatoes, sliced
5 cm/2 in piece cucumber, sliced
few lettuce leaves
100 g/4 oz Country Pâté or
pork rillettes

baguettes

Country Pâté

cucumber

tomatoes

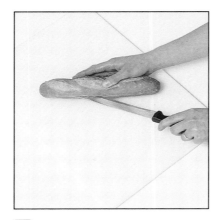

1 Cut the demi-baguettes three-quarters of the way through horizontally and spread the cut sides with butter.

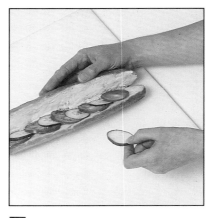

2 Fill with a layer of tomato and cucumber slices.

3 Lay the lettuce leaves over the top.

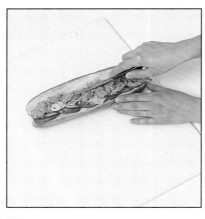

4 Spoon half the rillettes or pâté into each baguette and press together firmly.

COUNTRY PÂTÉ

Makes about 900 g/2 lb

225 g/8 oz streaky bacon rashers
 (slices), rind removed
350 g/12 oz/3 cups minced (ground)
 pork
225 g/8 oz pig's liver, minced
 (ground)
100 g/4 oz pork sausagemeat
1 onion, finely chopped
2 garlic cloves, crushed
5 ml/1 tsp chopped fresh thyme
15 ml/1 tbsp chopped fresh parsley
salt and pepper

Preheat the oven to 170°C/325°F/gas mark 3. Stretch the bacon with a palette knife (spatula) and use three-quarters of it to line a 900 ml/1½ pint/3¾ cup terrine. Set the remaining bacon aside.

Put the rest of the ingredients in a bowl and mix together thoroughly, or combine them in a food processor. Turn into the terrine and smooth the top. Cover with the remaining bacon.

Cover with a lid, or foil, and place in a roasting tin (roasting pan) half-filled with water and cook in the oven for 1¼–1½ hours.

Remove the lid or foil, cover with greaseproof paper (baking parchment), place a 1 kg/2¼ lb weight on top and leave until cold.

BRIE AND TOMATO BAGUETTE

Put a little lettuce and a few tomato slices in the baguette, then top with 50 g/2 oz ripe Brie slices and a few and stoned (pitted) black olives.

Herring and Apple on Rye

You can use rollmops, herrings in wine sauce or any other pickled herrings you like.

Makes 4

INGREDIENTS
25 g/1 oz/2 tbsp softened butter
4 slices rye bread
few lettuce leaves
4 pickled herring fillets
1 red apple, cored and sliced
5 ml/1 tsp lemon juice
60 ml/4 tbsp Fennel and Soured
   Cream Dressing
fennel sprigs, to garnish

rye bread

lettuce

apples

pickled herring

fennel

1 Spread the butter on the bread and cover with a few lettuce leaves.

2 Cut the herring fillets in half and arrange on top.

3 Brush the apple slices with lemon juice and arrange round the herring.

4 Spoon over some Fennel and Soured Cream Dressing and garnish with fennel.

HERRING, POTATO AND GHERKIN (DILL PICKLE)

Put 15 ml/1 tbsp potato salad on a lettuce leaf, arrange a herring fillet on top and garnish with sliced gherkin (dill pickle) and cherry tomatoes. Top with a fennel sprig.

BEETROOT, HERRING AND ONION

Put some sliced cooked beetroot over the lettuce, arrange a herring fillet on top and garnish with thinly sliced onion rings, Fennel and Soured Cream Dressing and a fennel sprig.

Ham and Asparagus Slice

Be creative in your arrangement of the ingredients here. You could make ham cornets, or wrap the asparagus in the ham, or use different meats such as salami, mortadella or Black Forest ham.

Makes 4

INGREDIENTS
12 asparagus spears
100 g/4 oz/½ cup cream cheese
4 slices rye bread
4 slices ham
few leaves curly endive
30 ml/2 tbsp mayonnaise
4 radish roses, to garnish

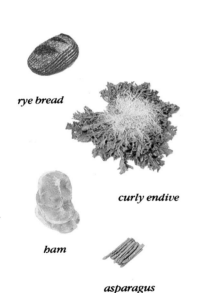

rye bread

curly endive

ham

asparagus

1 Cook the asparagus until tender, drain, pat dry with kitchen paper and cool.

2 Spread cream cheese over the rye bread and arrange the ham in folds over the top.

3 Lay 3 asparagus spears on each sandwich.

4 Arrange curly endive on top of the spears and spoon over some mayonnaise.

5 Garnish with radish roses and serve extra mayonnaise separately in a small bowl if liked.

SALAMI AND COTTAGE CHEESE SLICE

Omit the asparagus. Arrange 3 salami slices on top with a spoonful of cottage cheese and chopped fresh chives. Garnish with watercress, chives and chive flowers.

Scrambled Egg and Tomato Fingers

Pumpernickel makes a good firm base for these finger sandwiches and its flavour combines especially well with that of scrambled egg.

Makes 6

INGREDIENTS
25 g/1 oz/2 tbsp softened butter
2 slices pumpernickel bread
2 eggs
15 ml/1 tbsp milk
salt and pepper
15 ml/1 tbsp single (light) cream
30 ml/2 tbsp chopped fresh chives
mustard and cress
3 canned anchovy fillets, halved
2 sun-dried tomatoes, cut into strips
tomato rose and spring onion
    (scallion) tassel, to garnish

pumpernickel bread

eggs   *anchovy fillets*

mustard and cress

sun-dried tomatoes

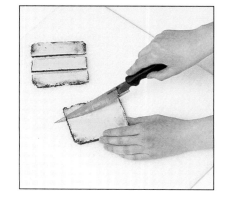

1 Butter the pumpernickel and cut into 6 fingers.

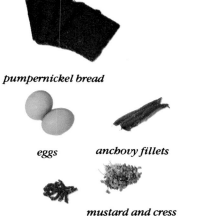

2 Whisk the eggs lightly with the milk and add seasoning to taste. Cook the eggs in a little melted butter over a gentle heat, stirring constantly until lightly scrambled.

3 Stir in the cream and chives, and leave to cool.

4 Arrange a little mustard and cress at the ends of the pumpernickel fingers and spoon over the egg. Place the anchovies and sun-dried tomato strips on top of the egg. Garnish with a tomato rose and spring onion (scallion) tassel.

Smoked Salmon and Gravlax Sauce

Gravlax is cured fresh salmon: it is marinated in dill, salt and sugar and left for 2–3 days with weights on it. It can be bought now in most supermarkets and delicatessens and you can use it instead of smoked salmon if you wish.

Makes 8

INGREDIENTS
25 g/1 oz/2 tbsp softened butter
5 ml/1 tsp grated lemon zest
4 slices rye or pumpernickel bread
100 g/4 oz smoked salmon
few leaves curly endive
lemon slices
cucumber slices
60 ml/4 tbsp Gravlax Sauce
dill sprigs, to garnish

curly endive

cucumber

lemon

smoked salmon

rye bread   *dill*

1 Mix the butter and lemon zest together, spread over the bread and cut in half diagonally.

2 Arrange the smoked salmon over the top to cover.

3 Add a little curly endive and a lemon or cucumber slice. Spoon over some Gravlax Sauce, then garnish with dill.

Tapenade and Quails' Eggs

Tapenade, a purée made from capers, olives and anchovies, is an excellent partner to eggs. Of course you can use hens' eggs, but quails' eggs look very pretty on open sandwiches.

Makes 8

INGREDIENTS
8 quails' eggs
1 small baguette
45 ml/3 tbsp Tapenade
few leaves curly endive
3 small tomatoes, sliced
4 canned anchovy fillets, halved
   lengthways
black olives
parsley sprigs, to garnish

baguette

curly endive

Tapenade

tomatoes

quails' eggs

1 Boil the quails' eggs for 5 minutes, then plunge straight into cold water to cool. Crack the shells and remove them very carefully.

2 Cut the baguette into diagonal slices and spread with some Tapenade.

3 Arrange curly endive and tomato slices on top.

4 Halve the quails' eggs and place over the tomato.

5 Finish with a little more Tapenade, the anchovies and olives. Garnish with small parsley sprigs.

TAPENADE

Makes 300 ml/10 fl oz/1¼ cups

Put a 90 g/3½ oz can drained tuna fish in a food processor with 25 g/1 oz capers, 10 canned anchovy fillets and 75 g/3 oz/¾ cup stoned (pitted) black olives and blend until smooth, scraping down the sides as necessary. Gradually add 60 ml/4 tbsp olive oil through the feeder tube and mix well.

Roquefort and Pear

Roquefort is delicious served with pear, but other blue cheeses such as Stilton or Cambozola can be used instead. Toasted brioche makes a good base but must be eaten straight away as it quickly becomes soft once filled.

Makes 4

INGREDIENTS
4 slices brioche loaf
125 g/4 oz/½ cup curd (smooth
   cottage) cheese
few sprigs rocket (arugula)
125 g/4 oz Roquefort cheese, sliced
1 ripe pear, quartered, cored and
   sliced
juice of ½ lemon
4 pecan nuts, to garnish
viola flowers, to garnish (optional)

curd (smooth cottage) cheese

pears

rocket (arugula)

pecan nuts

Roquefort cheese

1 Toast the brioche and spread with the curd (smooth cottage) cheese.

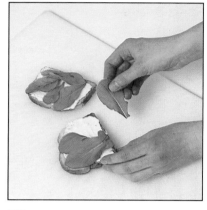

2 Arrange rocket (arugula) leaves on top of the cheese.

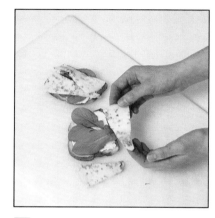

3 Place the sliced Roquefort on top.

4 Brush the pear slices with lemon juice to prevent discoloration.

5 Arrange the pear slices, overlapping, in a fan shape on the cheese.

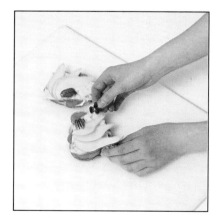

6 Garnish with pecan nuts (whole or chopped) and a viola flower if you wish.

PARTY SANDWICHES

Sandwich Train

This is a simple way to make sandwiches more appealing to small children, who can sometimes be difficult to please.

Makes 2 trains

INGREDIENTS
2 sandwich rounds made with soft
   filling
cucumber skin
radishes
a little sandwich filling
1 celery stick
1 carrot
1 cooked beetroot
cream cheese, lettuce and pretzel
   stick, to garnish (optional)

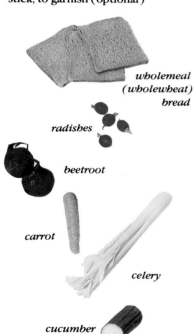

wholemeal (wholewheat) bread

radishes

beetroot

carrot

celery

cucumber

1 Remove the crusts from the sandwiches and cut each one into 4 squares.

2 Cut the squares in half again to make 8 small sandwiches.

3 Make an engine using 3 of the sandwiches. Arrange the remaining sandwiches behind the engine, placing cucumber strips to resemble tracks.

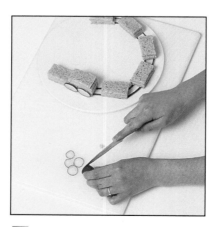

4 Slice the radishes and stick on to the sides of the train with a little sandwich filling to resemble wheels.

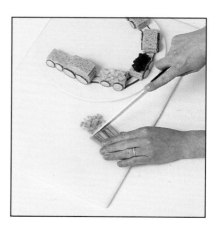

5 Dice the celery, carrot and beetroot and pile on to the trucks (freight cars) to resemble cargo.

6 Cut a carrot funnel, top with cream cheese smoke if liked and place on the engine with half a radish, and a piece of cucumber. If you want to make a tree, tie some lettuce onto a pretzel stick and stick it in position with a blob of cream cheese.

Log Cabin

This takes a little time but is a great favourite with children.

Makes 1

INGREDIENTS
4 sandwich rounds made with chosen filling, crusts removed
pretzel sticks
50 g/2 oz/¼ cup curd (smooth cottage) cheese
1 tomato
1 carrot
1 radish
2.5 cm/1 in piece cucumber

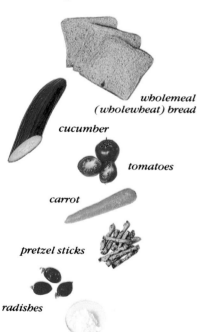

wholemeal (wholewheat) bread

cucumber

tomatoes

carrot

pretzel sticks

radishes

curd (smooth cottage) cheese

1 Place 2 of the sandwich rounds on a board and cut each into small rectangular sandwiches.

2 Cut each of the remaining 2 sandwich rounds into 4 triangles.

3 Stack the rectangular sandwiches together to form the cabin and place 6 of the triangles on top to form the roof. (Serve the rest of the triangles separately.)

4 Arrange pretzel sticks on the roof to look like logs, sticking with a little sandwich filling or curd (smooth cottage) cheese if necessary.

5 Break the remaining pretzel sticks into 2.5 cm/1 in lengths and use to make a fence around the cabin, sticking in position with curd cheese.

6 Cut the tomatoes into doors and windows. Cut the carrot into a chimney, attach it using curd cheese and add some curd cheese smoke. Cut flowers from radishes and carrots. Dice the cucumber finely and arrange on the plate to resemble a path.

Sailing Sandwich

A novelty shape may tempt even the most awkward child. The basic sandwich shape is quick and easy to make, though it's a bit more time-consuming to add the trimmings.

Makes 1

INGREDIENTS
1 sandwich round made with chosen
 filling
butter
chopped fresh parsley
few pretzel sticks
paprika
shredded lettuce
tomato ketchup and small pieces of
 lemon rind and cucumber, to
 garnish (optional)

lettuce

*wholemeal
(wholewheat) bread*

pretzel sticks

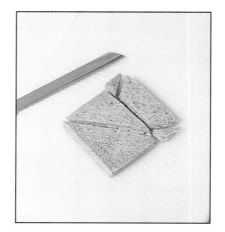

1 Remove the crusts from the sandwich and cut 2 triangular sails from it. Shape the remaining piece of sandwich to resemble a boat.

2 Spread the long edges of the sails with a little butter and dip in chopped parsley.

3 Turn one sail over and arrange 2 sides together with the pretzel sticks in the centre to represent the mast.

4 Spread the boat shape with butter, dip into paprika and place below the sails. Arrange shredded lettuce underneath to represent the sea. If liked, you can pipe a number on the sail with tomato ketchup. Cut out a sun from lemon rind and a flag from cucumber.

Sailing Ships

A novelty sandwich that you can prepare with different fillings. The processed cheese slices make wonderful sails.

Makes 12

INGREDIENTS
6 bridge rolls
225 g/8 oz chosen filling
chopped fresh parsley
2 tomatoes, quartered and seeded
2 radishes
6 processed cheese slices

bridge rolls

tomatoes

cheese slices

chives

I Cut each roll in half horizontally and trim the base so that it stands evenly. Put 15 ml/1 tbsp of the filling on to each half and spread to the edges, doming it slightly. Surround the filling with a border of chopped parsley if you like.

2 Cut the tomatoes into thin strips and arrange round the edge of each half-roll.

3 Cut the radishes into strips and 2 triangles. Cut the cheese into sail shapes. Thread each sail on to a cocktail stick (toothpick) and stand in the filling, supporting it with radish strips if necessary.

PEANUT FILLING
Mix together 45 ml/3 tbsp crunchy peanut butter and 45 ml/3 tbsp tomato chutney.

CHEESE AND PINEAPPLE FILLING
Thoroughly combine 100 g/4 oz/½ cup curd (smooth cottage) cheese, 30 ml/2 tbsp drained and chopped canned pineapple and add seasoning to taste.

Wigwams

Choose a square-shaped loaf, either brown or white, so that you can cut even-sized triangles; the bread should be thinly sliced.

Makes 4

INGREDIENTS
4 rounds sandwiches
butter
chopped fresh parsley
mustard and cress, or flat-leaf parsley
shredded lettuce
1 red (bell) pepper (optional)
pretzel sticks (optional)

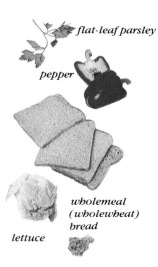

flat-leaf parsley

pepper

wholemeal (wholewheat) bread

lettuce

mustard and cress

1 Cut each sandwich into triangles.

2 Cut a slanting slice from the base of each triangle so that the sandwich will stand at an angle.

3 Butter one or two of the long sides of the triangles and dip in chopped parsley.

4 Place 4 triangles together to form a wigwam shape.

5 Arrange a small bunch of mustard and cress or flat-leaf parsley to fit in between the sandwiches at the top. Around the base of the wigwam arrange shredded lettuce and, if liked, strips of red (bell) pepper cut zig-zag fashion along one edge. Pretzel sticks may be added to represent poles.

ANIMAL SHAPES

Chill the sandwiches to make cutting easier. Use shaped cutters to make animals, stars, crescents or hearts as liked. Put a piece of radish on each sandwich to represent an eye or, in the case of a butterfly, a body.

Smoked Salmon Pinwheels

Use a small, fresh, unsliced loaf for these so that you can cut the bread lengthways and achieve a reasonable-sized pinwheel. The bread is easier to slice if it is half-frozen.

Makes 56

INGREDIENTS
1 small unsliced brown loaf
1 small lemon
75 g/3 oz/6 tbsp softened butter
15 ml/1 tbsp chopped fresh dill
225 g/8 oz smoked salmon slices
black pepper

brown loaf　*lemons*

smoked salmon

dill

1 Slice the loaf carefully along its length into 8 thin slices. Cut off the crusts.

2 Grate the lemon zest finely and mix together with the butter and dill.

3 Spread on each slice and arrange smoked salmon over the bread to cover, leaving a strip of buttered bread at one short end. Grind some black pepper over the top.

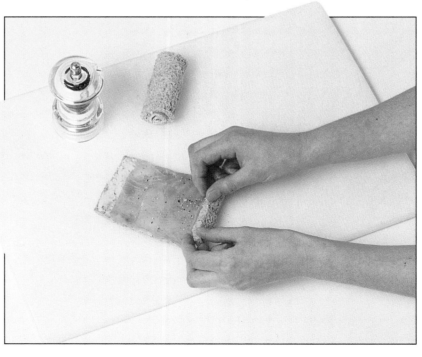

4 With the salmon-covered short end towards you, roll up the bread carefully and tightly, like a Swiss (jelly) roll. The buttered end will ensure the bread sticks together.

5 Wrap in clear film (plastic wrap) and chill for 1 hour. This will help the filling and bread to set in the rolled position and ensure that it does not unwind on slicing. Repeat with the remaining slices.

6 Using a sharp knife, cut each roll into 1 cm/½ in slices.

Asparagus Rolls

Use green asparagus as it is usually thinner and looks more attractive. A 340 g/12 oz can usually contains about 20 spears.

Makes 20

INGREDIENTS
20 slices wholemeal (wholewheat) bread, crusts removed
100 g/4 oz/½ cup softened butter
salt and pepper
350 g/12 oz can asparagus tips, drained
lemon slices and fresh flowers, to garnish

black pepper

wholemeal
(wholewheat) bread

asparagus

butter

1 Roll the bread lightly with a rolling pin (this makes it easier to roll up without cracking). Mix the butter and seasoning and spread over each slice of bread.

2 Lay an asparagus tip at one end of the bread with the tip overlapping slightly. Roll up tightly like a Swiss (jelly) roll and press the end so that the butter sticks it together.

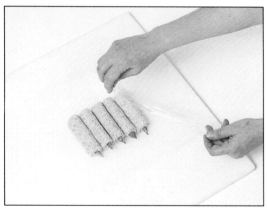

3 Pack the rolls tightly together, wrap in clear film (plastic wrap) and chill for 1 hour so that they set in a rolled position and do not unwind when served. Serve garnished with lemon slices and fresh flowers if liked.

Striped Sandwiches

These are rather fragile when cut, so be sure to chill them for a couple of hours before slicing. To achieve a more contrasting effect you may like to add a little green colouring to the Cheese and Chive Filling.

Makes 32

INGREDIENTS
6 slices brown bread
4 slices white bread
1 quantity Tuna and Tomato Filling
½ quantity Egg and Cress Filling
½ quantity Cheese and Chive Filling
cucumber slices, chives and fresh
    flowers, to garnish

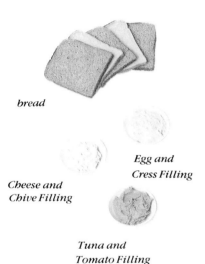

bread

*Egg and
Cress Filling*

*Cheese and
Chive Filling*

*Tuna and
Tomato Filling*

1 Start with a slice of brown bread and spread it with Tuna and Tomato Filling.

2 Place a white slice on top and spread with Egg and Cress Filling. Repeat with Cheese and Chive Filling, then the tuna again, using brown and white bread alternately. Repeat with the remaining fillings and bread. Wrap in foil and chill for 2 hours.

3 Unwrap, cut off the crusts and, using a sharp knife, cut into 1 cm/½ in slices. Cut the slices in half and serve garnished with cucumber slices, chives and fresh flowers if liked.

Sandwich Horns

These are good sandwiches for a party, but avoid using dry fillings. Smooth soft fillings, such as cream cheese, pâté or taramasalata, are most suitable. Use thinly sliced bread to make the shaping easier.

Makes 8

INGREDIENTS
8 thin slices bread
100 g/4 oz/½ cup cottage cheese
15 ml/1 tbsp mixed chopped fresh
    parsley, chives and thyme
salt and pepper
100 g/4 oz/½ cup each Avocado
Filling and Smoked Salmon Filling
few sprigs fresh herbs, to garnish

*wholemeal
(wholewheat) bread*

Avocado Filling

fresh herbs

1 Remove the crusts from the bread.

2 Cut one corner off each slice, rounding it slightly. For small horns cut a smaller square of bread.

3 Mix the cottage cheese and chopped herbs together with some seasoning. Spread the bread with about half of this mixture.

4 Lift the two sides and fold one over **the** other with the rounded area at the **base** of the horn. Stick the bread in position with the filling. Secure with a cocktail stick (toothpick) and chill for 20 minutes to firm up. Repeat using the Smoked Salmon Filling and Avocado Filling.

5 Hold the horn upright in one hand and spoon in the remaining filling.

SMOKED SALMON FILLING

Put 50 g/2 oz smoked salmon pieces in a blender with 75 ml/3 fl oz/⅓ cup double (heavy) cream, 5 ml/1 tsp lemon juice, and a little black pepper. Blend briefly – not too much or the cream will curdle. The result should be a rough purée.

6 Remove the cocktail stick before serving and garnish with a sprig of herbs.

Cucumber Sandwiches

These traditional afternoon-tea sandwiches are easy to prepare and always popular.

Makes 4

INGREDIENTS
½ cucumber
30 ml/2 tbsp white wine vinegar
50 g/2 oz/4 tbsp softened butter
8 slices white bread
salt and pepper

white bread

white wine vinegar

cucumber

butter

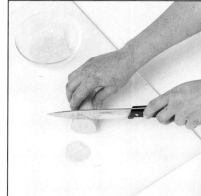

1 Cut a few thin slices of cucumber to use as a garnish and set aside, then peel the rest and slice thinly. Place in a bowl, pour over the vinegar and leave to marinate for 30 minutes. Drain well.

2 Butter the bread, arrange the cucumber slices over half the slices and sprinkle with salt and pepper.

3 Cover with the remaining buttered bread to make 4 sandwiches. Press together firmly and cut off the crusts. Cut each sandwich into 4 triangles and serve garnished with the cucumber slices.

WATERCRESS SANDWICHES

Finely chop 1 bunch watercress. Spread 60 ml/5 tbsp mayonnaise over 8 slices buttered wholemeal (wholewheat) bread. Arrange the watercress over 4 of the slices, season well and sandwich together with the remaining 4 slices.

Spicy Chicken Canapés

These tiny little cocktail sandwiches have a spicy filling, finished with different toppings. Use square bread so that you can cut more rounds and have less wastage from each sandwich.

Makes 18

INGREDIENTS
75 g/3 oz/⅓ cup finely chopped
  cooked chicken
2 spring onions (scallions), finely
  chopped
30 ml/2 tbsp chopped red (bell)
  pepper
90 ml/6 tbsp Curry Mayonnaise
6 slices white bread
15 ml/1 tbsp paprika
15 ml/1 tbsp chopped fresh parsley
30 ml/2 tbsp chopped salted peanuts

pepper

white bread

parsley

cooked chicken

*spring onions
(scallions)*

Curry Mayonnaise

1 Mix the chicken with the chopped spring onions (scallions) and red (bell) pepper and half the Curry Mayonnaise.

2 Spread the mixture over 3 of the bread slices and sandwich with the remaining bread, pressing well together. Spread the remaining Curry Mayonnaise over the top and cut into 4 cm/1 ½ in circles using a plain cutter.

3 Dip into paprika, chopped parsley or chopped nuts and arrange on a plate.

INDEX